The ABC's
Of
Living Skillfully

I AM MY FIRST PRIORITY

Sharon Lynn High Williams

Success doesn't happen all at once. It's a process of continual growth and development that starts and ends with you. Making yourself the priority in your story is the key to unlocking the greatness that's within you. Before you can ever hope to help and support the dreams of another, you have to first, accomplish all you've set out to do. Your goals matter. You matter. And, the sooner you recognize just how essential you are to the success of your story, the sooner you'll start heading down the road that leads to your personal fulfillment. Applied knowledge is power. Knowing, however, is not enough. What's most important is what you do with what you know. The ability to change your life for the better has always been in your hands. Let Sharon Williams' "The ABC's of Living Skillfully guide your next best steps forward as you prepare to live your best life, right now.

Eric D. Thomas, PhD. "ET, the Hip Hop Preacher"
Founder,
Eric Thomas & Associates, LLC.
Grand Ledge, MI 48837

Hello Independent Thinker,

This book has been written with the belief that inside of you is greatness waiting to burst forth. The skills tucked inside these pages were designed to assist you in managing your life in a way that will help you to be successful. There may be changes that you need to make but those changes will only make you a stronger individual.

I AM MY FIRST PRIORITY

The life you're living is the only one you're going to get.

It's necessary that you understand how important your life is and that everything you do has consequences that may affect the way you are allowed to live your life. At times, we take for granted how we are living our lives, and we allow chances to slip away without exploring their possibilities.

'I AM MY FIRST PRIORITY' is a **standard of behavior** that provides self-imposed guidelines to help you structure your daily living. In simplest terms, it means, 'I am learning to do what is in my best interest'. Don't worry, this is not an act of selfishness, but a statement of intent. Having a successful life isn't going to happen by accident; you must intentionally plan for it. It is necessary to have the right tools to help you navigate through life. Knowledge is power, and having the right tools will empower you, increase your confidence and your chances for success.

You must learn that you are the most important person in your world. It's not your friends or even family members; it must be you. When you are at your best, you attract like-minded people and your family and friends will be pleased with the direction of your life.

Greatness is in you, but it must be cultivated to grow and come forth. Allowing yourself to get into situations that bring negative consequences can hinder your growth and even cause setbacks that are difficult, if not impossible to overcome. It's time to be your own best friend. Say this, "I am my first priority".

"I Am My First Priority."

Table of Contents

ABOUT THE AUTHOR

Sharon High Williams is a Colorado native, happily married with a loving family. She has dedicated more than 40 years of her life to help children of all ages overcome their fears and open their young minds to the endless possibilities available to them. Being blessed with a daughter of her own, Sharon has expanded her motherly concerns for countless other children. She is a certified life coach and has worked with children from all walks of life including the ones in the judicial system, psychiatric facilities and churches. "Childhood is a time when children struggle to connect with others; socially and emotionally. In this technology driven age, it has become more difficult for them to connect on a personal level." Sharon teaches life skills to children to help them cope with the challenges of life. Through her lessons, she aims to give children the best gifts of their lives; confidence and self-respect. Sharon continues her mission to unveil the greatness in each child and empower them to live a strong, healthy and happy life.

DEDICATION

This book is dedicated to all the children GOD has allowed to cross my path. Each child adding something valuable to my life; which I in-turn shared with others. It's dedicated to the children who wanted a change in their lives and to those who weren't yet ready. It's dedicated to the children who worked on developing their futures and to those who will never have one. Shout out to the parents who are deliberately raising their children and a prayer for those who aren't. This book is also dedicated to my parents, Elmus Lee High, Sr. and Roberta Howard High for allowing me the chance to experience unconditional love; even when it was hard. Special thanks to my husbands, John W. Williams, Jr. for always supporting my dreams and to my daughter, Johniqua for being my iron. Also, thanks to Sheila, Jacquese & Denise.

A

A.C.T.

(attainable, challenging, time sensitive)

A.C.T. is a goal setting tool that lays out an easy pattern to follow. Setting goals is vital to personal growth and allows you to experience success on different levels. Goal setting falls into two categories: immediate and long term. When setting goals, they should be:

- **ATTAINABLE –** When you start setting goals, make sure they aren't so outrageous that there's no possible way you will reach them; like jumping rope on mars. This causes frustration and discourages you from trying.

- It is important that the goals you're setting are **CHALLENGING**. There is a thin line between attainable and challenging. A goal that challenges you should push you out of your comfort zone and cause your imagination to step out of the box and allow you to have new experiences. Procrastination or putting

3

things off, is the enemy of new ideas and is a trap that sneaks up on you and gobbles up your time.

- Being **TIME SENSITIVE** means setting specific dates and time lines; this also allows you to envision when the project is complete. As the deadline approaches, periodically review your progress to ensure that you're on schedule; this works well with homework.

AFFIRMATIONS

As a skill, affirmations are positive statements that encourage and motivate us and are often derived from casual statements we may have heard throughout our lives. The most powerful affirmations come from reversing negative statements that have been said to us or about us.

List three positive statements that encourage or motivate you:

(*Example: I will not allow others to define me. I am uniquely made.*)

_____

_____

_____

We all have a tape playing in our heads that speaks to who we are. There are usually several contributors; some welcomed and others not. The messages on this tape have the power to influence us in a negative and positive way. In order to operate effectively under our **Standard of Behavior**, it is important that we identify the negative messages and then create a positive one to replace it, we call this the 'override'.

List three negative or hurtful statements that have influenced your life.

(*Example: You're not very smart. You never do anything right.*)

_____

_____

_____

Now create an override for each negative statement:

Override: _____

_____

_____

Override: _____

_____

_____

Override: _____

_____

_____

As a tool this skill can be used at any time. The affirmations should be memorized so that they become part of you and can be called upon whenever you need them. It would be helpful to place each of your affirmations on index card to help you learn and memorize them.

Use the spaces to get you started with your affirmations.

(*It will be helpful to get a pack of index cards and create your set of affirmations*)

I Am My First Priority; I'm learning to do what is in my best interest.	

Exercise: Affirmations can always be helpful. Daily use of affirmations will keep you encouraged and add a nice moment to each day. This exercise is called **'Fill My Cup'**. Get a disposable coffee cup with a lid (decorate it if you like). Use strips of paper and write out one affirmation a day, for thirty days and place it in the cup. At the end of the thirty days you'll have a full cup. From that point on, you can open the cup and read as many affirmations as you'd like when you need them. There is no limit to how many affirmations you put in the cup. Once you've read them, put them back for use another day.

AGREE TO DISAGREE

We all have had different experiences and established different beliefs. It is not realistic to think that you are going to get along with everyone. With this in mind, we have to make sure that we don't let our differences erupt into a problem. There are three R's for you to remember when you're in a situation where you just can't agree with what's being said or done.

1. Respect

2. Realize

3. Remove

It is always important to <u>respect</u> the views and opinions of other; even if you can't agree. It is equally important that you <u>realize</u> that continuing the discussion isn't going to change things. Finally, <u>remove</u> yourself from the situation to avoid the possibility of things escalating.

ANGER MANAGEMENT & ANGER SEQUENCE

Anger is a natural human emotion. The problem arises when we allow our anger to control us instead of us controlling it. The origin of anger is not our focus, just know that much of your anger is connected to other feelings. We're going to identify what your anger looks like and develop strategies and skills to address it.

Describe your behavior when you're at your angriest.

_____

_____

_____

Triggers:

Triggers are situations or circumstances that cause you to react. *For example, if someone were to call you a bad name; that would make you act or react to what was said.* It is important that you begin to understand when you are being or have been triggered. It is also important to pay attention to how your body is responding.

Identify five (5) of your triggers:

1. _____

2. _____

3. _____

4. _____

5. _____

Body cues:

It is said that self-preservation is the first law of nature. Body cues are your body's way of alerting you once you have been triggered. Body cues range from sweaty palms to a dry mouth to an increase in body temperature. Each person has their own set of body cues. As the body cues continue, anger is increasing; headed for the point of no return. Before anger reaches its maximum level, it is necessary to interrupt the sequence. (*For example, your palms may become sweaty, your breathing may change, ears burn etc.*)

Identify your body's reactions when you've been triggered:

(List in order of occurrence)

```
_____          _____
_____          _____
_____          _____
_____          _____
_____          _____
```

Within the body cues, there is a point of no return. This is that point where there's no stopping the anger from going full blown. It is necessary to insert coping skills early enough in the sequence to prevent it from reaching maximum strength.

Anger Sequence:

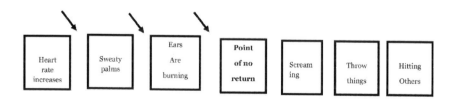

Between the first three body cues are where coping skills need to be inserted before the emotions are out of control. As you learn more about coping skills, you will gain an understanding of how the skills work best. As you get closer to the 'point of no return', the intensity of the coping skill should increase so that the chances of going past the 'point of no return' lessens. As you get further in this book you will learn coping skills that will help with anger and can be inserted into the anger sequence.

ATTITUDES

Isn't it funny that nobody really notices your attitude until it becomes negative? It's as if a negative attitude creeps up on you without your permission. Understand that your attitude helps to determine how others will react to you. It is true that misery loves company but individuals who are trying to have a productive life will not want to be around the negativity; and you don't want to be the source of it.

ATTITUDE CHECK:

(In the mornings as you're starting your day, ask yourself these questions.)

- How do I want this day to go?
- How am I feeling right now?
- What are three positive things I can do to start my day?
- What are three negative things to avoid?
- What affirmation can I carry into this day? *(write it on paper and place it in your pocket or backpack)*

This is just a guideline, but it will point you in the right direction. If at some point in the day you feel as though your attitude has become negative, take a moment to yourself and review the affirmation(s) you chose earlier in the day. It is also necessary to look at what has affected your mood or attitude. By doing this you are helping yourself to be more prepared when facing similar situations.

A.W.E.

This coping skill works hand-in-hand with the **Standard of Behavior. Accept Without Excuses**. Remember that the 'Standard of Behavior states that, "I am my first priority'. What that means is, 'I am learning to do what is best for me'. A.W.E. is utilized when you're faced with a situation you know is not good for you. Instead of trying to find a loop hole, remember your Standard of Behavior and, because you realize that the situation is not in your best interest all you can say is A.W.E. and accept it without excuses.

B

BEHAVIOR

Your behaviors tell the story of YOU. Others watch your behaviors and come to a decision about who you are or aren't. Part of living; according to your 'Standard of Behavior', is learning to take charge of YOU. Parents and teachers will give you guidelines and instructions but then it is up to you to decide whether you're going to follow them. What does your behaviors say about you and is it what you want to be said?

List five of your behaviors; positive and negative, and share what you think those behaviors say about you. (*If you're not sure, ask a parent, a teacher, or a friend*)

Positive Behaviors:	What does it say about you?
(*Name the Behavior*)	(*Name the Behavior*)

Negative Behaviors:	What does it say about you?
(*Name the Behavior*)	(*Name the Behavior*)

BOUNDARIES

Keeping our 'Standard of Behavior' in mind, it is important that you set your own boundaries. Boundaries are personal limits put in place to help you keep yourself safe and to respect others. We're going to focus on three boundary categories: **physical, verbal** and **social**.

- **Physical –** Physical boundaries are related to your physical body. Stand up and stretch out your arms, then turn around. The space from the tip of your fingers to your body's core is your personal bubble. This space is private and should not be entered without your permission. You must remember that others have the same bubble and you shouldn't enter their space without permission. If someone does violate your space, you do have the right to tell them to stop and if necessary you can report this to a person in authority (parent, teachers, or police).

- **Verbal –** Verbal boundaries are related to our conversations. The type of conversation you have is based on who you're talking with. The information you would share with a family member or trusted friend, isn't the same as the information you would share with someone you've just met. Your business is just that; yours. You must understand your value and not give pieces of you away by sharing too much of yourself with individuals that don't need to have that information. Verbal boundaries also include conversations with the opposite sex. Intimate details about yourself or your past are to be shared on a need to know basis, and you're the one that decides who needs to know; not them.

- **Social** – Manners, or how you conduct yourself in public speaks volumes about who you are or who you will be perceived to be. There are different rules for different places, but you need to have your own personal set of guidelines about how you behave yourself. Being rude isn't an option. If you encounter difficulty, use the skills you're learning to address the situation. There is no shame in using the words 'please and thank you'. People would rather deal with a pleasant person than a rude grumpy one. Also, be mindful of your volume; being loud has its place but shouldn't be a part of your regular routine

C

C.H.O.I.C.E.

One of the main things you should get out of this book is that you have the right and ability to choose who you are becoming and the direction you need to take in your life. The choices you make now may affect you for years to come, so you must pay attention to the choices you make.

C - Control – Don't live reckless. Be aware of the 'Ooops factor' and be deliberate about your actions.

H- How – The 'how' is the methods that you use to make choices which are in your best interest. As you go through this book you will learn different methods for making decisions. Use your skills.

O - Orderly – Develop steps or a quick process for getting from point 'A to point 'B'. For example: You're in a situation where those around you are doing something that you know is wrong for you. Once you decide how you are going to respond, you must put your plan together. Example: 1. Get my coat. 2. Call a parent. 3. Leave the area. Plans may vary depending on the situation.

I - I – This of course means you. Remember, you are your first priority.

C - Care – How much you care is dependent upon the level of the situation's importance, which can take on different priorities and should be addressed based on their urgency.

E - Engage – Act without procrastination. When you are putting things off, there is a tendency not to complete them, or to complete them in a rush and not as thorough.

CIRCLE OF INFLUENCE

The circle of influence is a group of people that you allow to be part of your life. These are people you respect, listen to, and may take advise from. Understand that you have given them a great privilege and responsibility that shouldn't be taken lightly. When developing your 'circle of influence', you need to fill these four basic positions: confidant, confronter, the jokester and the intellect.

- **The confidant** is someone that you trust and can share your thoughts and feelings with. One of their greatest qualities is their ability to listen.

- **The confronter** is someone that will tell you the truth about yourself; even if you don't want to hear it. This person has your best interest in mind and isn't scared off if you become upset about what they may say.

- **A 'jokester** is someone that makes you laugh because they can offer you a fresh perspective on different situations.

- **The Intellect** is someone you know is smarter than you. They will challenge you to be and do better.

In the diagram, fill in the names of the person that fills the roles identified. Your name goes in the middle.

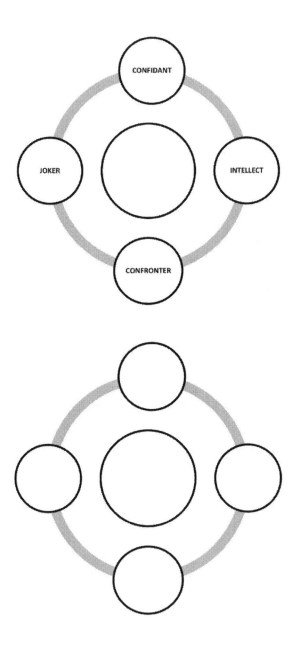

COME TO YOUR SENSES

We're all familiar with the five senses: sight, hearing, touch, taste and smell. However, we are not in the habit of using them as coping skills. It is important to remember that the art of using coping skills is to know which skill to use at what time. **Come To Your Senses**, is a skill that can be used to help you calm down when angry or anxious.

Sight - 'Eye Spy' is the name of the game. Look around you and see how many of the same color items you can find. Go through several colors before moving on to hearing.

Hearing - Do you hear what I hear? Silence yourself. Listen and identify the sounds around you. Once you run out of sounds, move on to touch.

Touch - Without looking, use your finger tips to run along the nearest surface. Be mindful of every change you feel along the surface until you can imagine what the change looks like. You can do this to different surfaces.

Taste - This one is not as easy to use as the others. One way is by using gum, mints or candy; focus on the taste and the texture.

Smell - This skill can be as simple as scented candles or a specific hand lotion. The point is to use a pleasant scent that will work to calm you when needed. Lavender is very popular.

C.O.M.M.O.N. vs U.N.C.O.M.M.O.N.

Your uniqueness is your gift to the world. Too often it is easier to try and be like everybody else so that you can fit in. The only problem with that is that YOU never fit in when you're changing to be something you're not. Denying your own uniqueness in order to be like others only makes you **COMMON.**

- **C –** Counterfeit
  - o Not your true self. Anything that is counterfeit is always of lesser value than the original.
- **O –** Ordinary

- o Nothing special. This doesn't allow you to find your unique beauty because you've settled.

- **M – Mimics others**

  - o Being what you imagine others to be. Unfortunately, they're faking it too.

- **M – Mediocre**

  - o Less than your best. It's impossible to be at your best when you're trying to be like somebody else.

- **O – Obstinate**

- o Being stubborn. When you're unwilling to look at possibly changing, which causes you to be stuck where you are.

- **N – Narrow minded**

  - o Limited point of view. Refusing to look beyond your comfort zone to new possibilities.

Why settle for being common when being **UNCOMMON** has so many great possibilities. This is an opportunity to get to know yourself better and to challenge yourself to be the best possible you.

- **U – Unique**

- o One of a kind. There is nobody like you; and that's a good thing because it allows you to make history.

- **N – Notable**
  - o Important. Who you are and the life you live is important and it matters that you are here and accomplishing your goals.

- **C – Courageous**
  - o Facing and overcoming difficult situations. Difficulties will come but you must understand that by pushing through those difficulties, and using your skills, you will make personal gains.

- **O – Occupied**
  - o Intentional busyness. Not wasting your time with thing that aren't beneficial to you.

- **M – Measuring**
  - o Acknowledging progress. Give yourself credit when you do well and encourage yourself to do better when things don't go right.

- **M – Motivated**
  - o Be encouraged to continue. Don't give up even during difficulties.

- **O – Obedient**

- o Following instructions. You are constantly being given directions on how to succeed. Following those instructions.

- **N – Nice**

- o Be kind. It cost nothing to show kindness but it could cost you everything if you're unkind.

COMMUNICATION SKILLS

It is important to develop your communication skills so you can represent yourself well in all situations. Being able to communicate well could be the difference in getting what you need and being misunderstood.

Goal of Communication:

The goal of communication is to get or give information effectively; knowing that it is going to cause some type of reaction.

VERBAL	NON-VERBAL
• Volume	• Appearance
• Tone of voice	• Attitude
• Specific words	• Body language

Verbal

Volume: Consider three basic volume levels: loud, medium, and soft. The loud volume may be used to get other's attention, or it may be considered aggressive. The soft volume may cause you to be perceived as weak. Most often the medium volume is preferred. All of this is dependent upon the type of situation you are in.

Tone of Voice: This is how you say what you say. You can say it nice or harsh. You can use humor or sarcasm. Either of these elements will determine how your information is received and the type of response you receive.

Specific Words: There are two parts to specific words. First is, use correct English: There is a time and place for slang. How you talk when you're with your friends is different than if you were talking with adults or in a professional setting. Second, say what you mean and mean what you say. Don't use words or phrases with double meaning; in an attempt to manipulate situations.

Non-Verbal

Appearance: There's an old saying that says, "you can't judge a book by it cover"; unfortunately, people still judge. How you look or what you wear, communicates a message. It is your responsibility to make sure that it's a message you want communicated

Attitude: Attitude is the posture or position of your body; along with your disposition.

Body Language: Your body will tell a story without your permission. It may come through a certain gestures or different postures. Something as simple as rolling your eyes or hunching your shoulders can send a message.

Barriers to effective 'communication'

A barrier is something that has the ability to stop or distract you from reaching your communication goals.

What are your distractions?

1. _____

2. _____

3. _____

4. _____

5. _____

Here are just a few pointers to remember:

- It is important for you to understand what you are communicating; verbally and non-verbally.

- You must begin to pay attention to what others are communicating to you; verbally and non-verbally.

CONFLICT RESOLUTION

Conflict is a natural part of life. As long as you're dealing with someone in addition to yourself, there is a potential for conflict. The trick is to know how to handle the conflict. Here are four skills to help you address any conflict you may face:

Accommodate: To allow a person to have their way, with the understanding that you'll get your way eventually.

Compromise: Making attempts to meet in the middle. This will require some negotiation, and it may be necessary for all involved to give up something in order to reach a compromise.

Collaborate: To collaborate is to gather information from a variety of sources in an effort to come up with the best possible answer.

Avoid: - This means do not address the conflict. 'Avoid' should be used when addressing a situation that would cause it to escalate.

COUNT & CHANT

'Count and Chant' is a skill you can use in a variety of places for a variety of situations. It's a simple formula:

Take a deep breath and hold it while counting down from five, (starting with your pinky). When you reach your thumb, sloooowly release your breath.

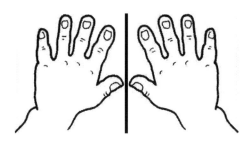

Repeat using the chant:

Take a deep breath and hold it. Starting with your pinky, say to yourself, "I – am – calming – myself – down. When you reach the thumb, release your breath.

Inhale and go to the left hand, "I – feel – myself – calming – down." When you reach the thumb, slowly release your breath.

Repeat the cycle if necessary.

D

DECISION MAKING

- How do you go about making decisions?
- Are your decisions based on how you're feeling at the moment?
- Do you take the time to think about what you're doing and why?
- Do you consider consequences?

Being able to make proper decisions is a powerful tool, and in order for you to be able to make solid decisions, you need your own personal decision-making process. Let's create your process:

Situation – When making a decision, it can be for a positive or a negative situation that needs to be addressed.

S.T.O.P. – The first thing you must do is to S.T.O.P.

- Silent
- Take a deep breath
- Organize your thoughts

- Proceed with a plan

Filter Questions – Filter questions are questions that you must ask yourself before making a decision. They work to sift situations through to help you come up with the best possible decision. Filter questions must be based on things that are important to you. (*Example: Will this decision cause my family not to trust me?*)

Now it's time for you to create your own set of filter questions. I will give you the first question.

1. Does this violate my Standard of Behavior?

2. _____

3. _____

4. _____

5. _____

6 _____

7_____

8_____

Rationalizing – Rationalizing is a way that we lie to ourselves in order to make a situation seem to be "not that bad". When there is a need to rationalize, it's because we know that what we're doing isn't 'quite' right but we still want to do it. However, you are usually violating your Standard of Behavior when you start rationalizing.

A.W.E. – Accept without excuses. Once you have gone through the filter questions and it comes out that this particular decision violates your standard of behavior, all you can say then is A.W.E. and accept that you can't do

E

ELEVATOR PITCH

An elevator pitch is defined as a short persuasive sales pitch. As far as using an elevator as a skill, it is very valuable when introducing yourself. It can be used in business or just to let someone know who you are. You can share your likes and information about what you're doing.

Create a quick elevator pitch about yourself:

I'm _____

_____

_____

_____

E.S.C.A.P.E.

Everyone needs an opportunity to escape at one time or another. E.S.C.A.P.E. is a skill that encourages you to take a moment for yourself. Many times, we're more concerned about taking care of others and we don't do the same for ourselves.

E – Exercise

S – Self

C – Care

Exercising self- care means to do something kind for yourself. Whatever you choose to do doesn't necessarily involve others, but it is a time of building yourself up. Take the time to do something you like.

A – And

P – Personal

E – Enhancement

Personal enhancement involves learning something new. The sky is the limit. Investigate a topic you want to know more about and keep track of what you're leaning so that you can always go back to it, as needed.

Take a minute to jot down five things you are interested in learning about.

1. _____

2. _____

3. _____

4. _____

5. _____

EXPECTATIONS

This may seem like an odd skill, but it is a necessary one. It is never too early to begin setting up self-expectations. Other people will always have expectations of you on some level; it begins with your parents. The question is, 'What do you expect from yourself?' The skill of Expectations requires that you set up general expectations for specific areas of your life, and include steps to reach your goals. These serve as a guideline for behaviors and decisions you may make.

Identify the expectations you currently have in these areas of your life.

My Behavior	Family Relationships	Friends	My Future
I expect to do my best.	*My family expects me to be honest.*	*I expect my friends to be loyal.*	*I expect to have a good job.*

As you grow and learn more about yourself and life in general, the expectations will shift.

F

F.A.I.L.U.R.E.

Failure is one of the greatest teachers we can possibly encounter. No one wants to fail, but if you're trying to have the best possible life, failure is going to happen. The key is to use your failures as teaching tools.

Failure occurs when:

Fear mixed with

Anger produces

Indifference and a

Lack of

Understanding and we become

Restricted by

Excuses

Make your failures work for you:

F -   **Focus:** Identify and avoid distractions.

A -   **Allow** yourself to make mistakes and then move on. When you make a mistake, don't waste time beating yourself up. Make a mental note of what you may have done wrong, make adjustments, and keep moving forward.

I -   **Influence:** Be deliberate about who and what you allow to influence your actions and decisions. Everything you do must be in your best interest.

L -   **Listen:** Listening is a skill that needs to be practiced. We usually want to do the talking. Silence yourself. When it comes to growing from failure, listen for better ideas and for areas you may have missed information.

U -   **Understanding** is key. When something goes wrong, or you don't meet your goals, take the time to get an understanding of what went wrong. This helps us not to repeat mistakes.

R -   <u>Review</u> the new plan. Make sure you're not repeating the same mistakes.

E -   <u>Engage:</u> Once you have gone through this failure sequence, it's time to try again.

FEAR

Fear can be crippling. The best remedy for fear is knowledge. It's our nature to fear what we don't understand and sometime that causes us to draw back and not investigate any further. However, if we will just begin to gather knowledge and get understanding about what caused us fear, we can overcome it. An important thing to understand is that you must be honest with yourself about what causes you to fear before you can face them. An option for addressing fear is to turn fear around. For example:

FEAR   **R.A.E.F.**

R –   **Review** the situation. What is really going on. What are you thinking? What are you feeling?

A –   **Assess** whether the fear is connected to your safety. Safety is always most important. Keep yourself safe.

E –   **Explore** your options for addressing the situation and identify any benefits you may be able to gain.

F –   **Face** the situation using your skills. Also ask questions and keep a record of your answers.

F.O.R.G.I.V.E.

All of us have experienced being hurt or mistreated. There may have been times when it was you who did the hurting or mistreating. Whatever the case may be, forgiveness is needed. A simple definition of forgiveness is: cease to feel resentment against an offender.

Misconceptions about forgiveness:

- Forgiveness gives the other person an advantage over you.
- Forgiving makes you look weak.

Truths about forgiveness:

- Forgiveness will benefit you.

- Forgiveness allows you to be free.

F - Freedom from negative feelings associated with an unpleasant or painful situation.

O - You have an **O**bligation to yourself to do what is in your best interest. Holding on to negative emotions is like walking around carrying weights and hoping the other person feels the discomfort.

R - When forgiveness happens, it opens the possibility of the **R**estoration of relationships. It also allows for the restoration of your peace of mind.

G - **G**ratitude is part of forgiveness because you should be grateful for the opportunity to mend wounds and possibly get things straight between yourself and someone who may have wronged you.

I - The act of forgiving is an **I**nvestment in yourself. To forgive is you taking care of you by not allowing anger and bitterness to set up in your heart. What's in our hearts will always come out in our behavior

V - Because unforgiveness brings with it a lot of negativity, to forgive adds **V**alue to your character. It's not easy to forgive, but just taking the necessary steps toward forgiving shows that you're a person with understanding and courage.

E - Esteem is the final element of 'forgive', because to forgive allows you the right to feel or think highly of yourself. To forgive is definitely an example of you maintaining your 'standard of behavior.'

Who do you need to forgive?

1. _____

2. _____

3. _____

F.R.E.E.Z.E

Sometimes when we are upset or irritated we're moving so quickly that we're not positioning ourselves to make good decisions. **FREEZE** is a coping skill that can be used when you need a moment to get yourself together. It's simple because it means just what it says; freeze.

F –   **FOCUS** on the situation you're dealing with. Look at it from different viewpoints.

R –   **REGROUP** and get control of self. Don't move or react until you have a clear understanding of what you're dealing with.

E –   **ESCAPE** is a mental time out; removing yourself away from the situation.

E –   **EMPLOY** coping skills as your next move.

Z –   **ZERO** in on a calming point. Find something in the area to fasten your eyes on, and take a few deep breaths.

E –   **ENGAGE** means to return to the situation. This should only be done once you know that you're in control of your behaviors and emotions.

FRIENDS

Friendship is a privilege, but the term 'friend' is over used and the relationship is often taken for granted. Consider the friends that you have.

Ask yourself:

- Why am I friends with this person?

- Do they make me better or worse?

- Do I add to their lives?

Your ultimate goal is to do what is in your best interest, so you must apply this concept when selecting friends. Friendships don't just happen, and it doesn't happen overnight. When considering your friends, don't under estimate your own value, and be clear on your reasons for friendship with any particular person.

Let's look at these three areas of relationships: associates, acquaintances and friends.

Acquaintance – A person you know but you're not close to. You may see this person on a regular basis but only have minimal interaction with them; no real connection. (*example: someone that you share classes with and acknowledge them in passing*)

Associates – A person that you share activities with. You are comfortable with them and enjoy their company. This may be a person you share your interests with and some of your personal opinions or thoughts. However, you don't share your inner personal information with.

Friend – This is a more personal relationship. This is a person you share yourself with and they share themselves with you. There is a connection or a bond that goes beyond shared interests.

An acquaintance could possibly grow into an associate and an associate can grow into a friend. One of the main elements is time, but what often happens is that you may try to make quick friends, or make friends for the wrong reasons.

It is important that you guard your heart and emotions. Make sure that the person you allow to become your friend deserves you and adds something positive to your life. You have a lot to offer; don't forget that!

This next exercise is an application for friendship. You may want to make several copies of this. You should fill one out for yourself because it will allow you to see what you bring to a friendship and it will help you to see what you're looking for in a friend. I encourage you to have a friend or someone you're considering to be your friend to fill one out too.

FRIEND APPLICATION

Name: _____ Age: _____

Nickname: _____

M or F Other (circle one)

Straight   Gay   Bi Not   sure (circle one)

Address:

_____

_____

Phone: _____ Email address: _____

How can you be reached on social media? _____

_____

Are you on Facebook? _____

Can I send you a friend request? _____

Are you on Instagram? _____

Who do you live with? _____

Do you have siblings? _____ How many? _____

What's your family like? _____

_____

_____

_____

Do you believe in GOD? _____ Explain _____

_____

_____

What are your beliefs? _____

_____

_____

Define friendship _____

_____

_____

What are you looking for in a friend? _____

_____

_____

What type of friend are you? _____

_____

_____

Are you a liar? _____

Do you like being lied to? _____

50

Explain: _____

_____

_____

Can you keep a secret? _____

What would make you tell a secret? _____

_____

_____

Have you ever been betrayed by someone you thought was a friend? _____

Explain: _____

_____

_____

Have you ever betrayed anyone? _____ Why? _____

_____

What makes you trustworthy? _____

What are your hobbies? _____

_____

Do you have a boyfriend/girlfriend? _____

What's their name? _____

Are you sexually active? _____

What type of books do you like? _____

Who is your favorite author? _____

What type of music do you like? _____

Who is your favorite singer? _____

What is your favorite song? _____

What are your future plans? _____

_____

What is something you hate to do? _____

_____

What kind of grades do you make? _____

_____

G

GRATITUDE

Gratitude is another way to say, "be thankful". It's always easy to find things that are wrong and when we do, our thoughts linger on them. Being grateful is a skill that can change your whole attitude, and help to change your perspective on negative or difficult situations. This will require practice because we are more accustomed to complaining than we are being grateful.

Gratitude Calendar

This exercise is to assist you in beginning to become a grateful person. On the grid provided, each day fill in the square with something that you're grateful for. Don't over think it. At the end of this exercise, share what you have learned.

What did you learn?

_____

_____

_____

_____

_____

_____

H

HAND WASHING

This is a skill that helps you to calm down and to refocus; while promoting good health. Start by massaging the palm of the hand and go down each finger while you concentrate on quoting the mantra below; start with the pinky. Slowly wash both hands. End with the thumb. It's important to use hand soap with a pleasing aroma.

Mantra:

- this is a small thing
- that I will not allow
- to become a big thing
- so, I release it
- into the atmosphere

I

INFLUENCE

Influence is the capacity or power of persons or things to be a compelling force on the behaviors and opinions of others. It is the producing of effects on a situation.

Earlier in this book you learned about the 'circle of influence' but when we talk about influence in this instance, this is more personal. Are you living a life that influences others and is it a positive or negative influence?

Here are a few questions to ask yourself.

1. What or who influences you to do well? _____

   _____

   _____

   _____

2. What influences you to do wrong? _____

   _____

   _____

   _____

3. Who do you influence, and how do you influence them? _____

_____

_____

_____

4. What influences you to change? _____

_____

_____

_____

5. How have you benefited from being influenced? _____

_____

_____

_____

INTEGRITY

Integrity isn't necessarily a skill but it's just as important. Integrity is keeping moral and ethical principles. A simpler way to say this is doing the right thing consistently; which is easy to say but not always easy to do. Maintaining your integrity speaks to the type of human being you are.

Integrity Check Up: (*ask yourself*)

- Am I being honest with myself and others?

- Am I keeping my word?

- Am I treating others the way I want to be treated?

The answers to these questions will help you see where you are and where you need to go in regard to being the person you want to be.

J

JOURNALING

Journaling is a skill that can be done in a variety of ways. It provides a way for you to get your thoughts and emotions out in a healthy way. I want to introduce you to four types of journaling: 90 seconds, situational, topical and dated.

> **90 seconds –** The type of journaling should take about a minute and a half. You write quickly and get out as much as you can; not necessarily on the issue that's irritating you. This is generally for individuals that don't like to write but need a quick release.

> **Situational –** This is used to write about a specific situation that you may be dealing with. The goal is to help sort out the situation in an effort to come up with a solution.

> **Topical –** This style of journaling is about a specific topic that isn't used too often but when it is, it is very detailed.

> **Dated –** This is the most commonly used type of journaling. It is meant to be used as a record of your life. Many use diaries for dated journaling.

K

KINDNESS

Kindness is a two-sided skill because it is administered two different ways. There's simple kindness and deliberate kindness.

Simple: This is kindness for kindness sake. There is no ulterior motive and is beneficial for both the giver and the receiver. Basically, it's just being nice to others. This directly effects how you feel about yourself, and you will begin to look for ways to show kindness to others.

Deliberate: This type of kindness is directed toward an individual that is mistreating you, or a situation that is not working in your favor. The kindness throws them off guard and it makes it more difficult for them to continue acting the same without looking foolish. This takes courage, and you can't be worried about what others may say about your actions.

L

LISTS

Lists are very helpful tools. When setting up your lists, there are a few specifics you should remember.

Lists are:

- Developed to get things done.
- Intended to keep you organized
- Be as detailed as you need them to be.

The key to insuring that the lists you create are beneficial, is to go back and check off what no longer needs to be on the list.

LYING

Lying. Don't do it! There may be times when it seems like lying is an option in order to keep yourself out of trouble, but don't do it. Your reputation is one of your most prize possessions and you don't want to tarnish it by lying. Lying becomes necessary when you haven't handled your business correctly; not doing what you're supposed to do when you're supposed to do it.

L – losing

Y – your

I – integrity

N – necessary to

G – grow into the individual you're trying to be.

The harm that one lie can do can never be predicted. It's like a weed that grows out of control; killing off positive growth. Lies destroy trust and damage relationships. Lying is absolutely not in your best interest.

M

MANNERS

'Please and thank you', are not dirty words! Having manners is a way of behaving that allows you to show respect for other people. When manners are used, it increases the chances of you being treated with respect. Everyone wants to be treated with respect, and for that to happen show respect.

MESSAGE VERIFICATION

Message verification simply means to make sure you understand the information being given.

Here's a formula to remember:

- The message is given.
- Repeat the information as you heard it.
- Listen for correction

- Re-word and repeat what you believe is being said. (*Example "What I hear you saying is….."*)

- Listen for verification.

MIND VACATION

Directing your mind to a place of serenity. This can be an actual place, or one created for the exercise. Make sure you are in a calm place and then begin your journey. All five senses will be used in this exercise. (*This skill works well with the Water Sipping skill, pg. 106*).

- **Sight -** Describe what you see in your calm place, be specific.(*Example: deep blue sky with billowy large white clouds*)

- **Hear -** Listen for the sounds around you and describe them in detail.(*Example: The birds singing and the wind in the trees*)

- **Feel -** What do you feel with your hands or against your skin. (*Example: warm sun on the skin or sand between your toes*)

- **Taste -** This can be something in your mouth or the air (*Example:salty air....*)

- **Smell -** This is any aroma in your peaceful place. (*Example: scented candles*)

MOTIVATORS

What motivates you? What gets you moving? It is important that you know the things that encourage you to move forward as well as the things that will hinder your forward movement. Motivators can be people, things or situations. Below list five (5) things that motivate you, and why:

1. _____
   _____

2. _____
   _____

3. _____
   _____

4. _____
   _____

5. _____

_____

Just like it's important to know what motivates you, it's equally important to know the things that discourage you. Below list five (5) things that discourage you, and what you need to do to avoid them:

1. _____

_____

2. _____

_____

3. _____

_____

4. _____

_____

5. _____

_____

N

NAVIGATING

This skill is a call to action. We have a tendency to talk about things for a long time before we start working on them. Navigate means move and move skillfully. When it comes to navigating you are going to be plotting your course. Paper and pencil are needed to write out your plans and the directions that need to be followed in order to reach the goal that you are trying to attain. Navigating well gives direction and allows you to see the progress you're making.

These are the steps to navigating well:

- Identify the goal.

- Identify the first step.

- Create a time line. This may shift over time.

- Identify tools or skills needed to reach goal. Gather the tools and begin to practice the skills.

- Take the first step, then identify the next two steps

- Monitor progress by looking for great and small changes, then ask yourself if the changes are headed in the direction you want to go.

- As you make progress, identify the upcoming steps until you reach your goal.

(See the navigation layout)

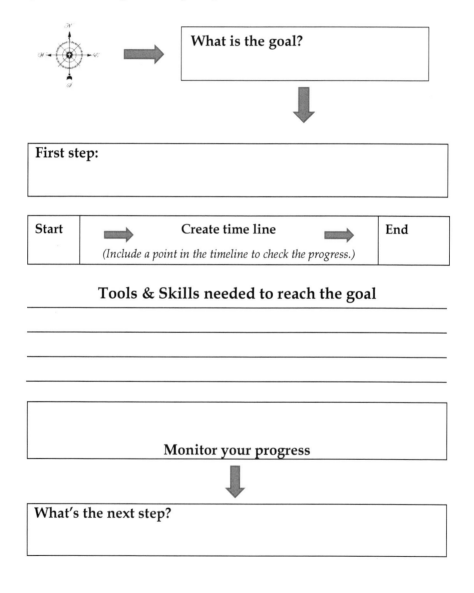

| | What is the goal? |

First step:

Start	Create time line	End
	(Include a point in the timeline to check the progress.)	

Tools & Skills needed to reach the goal

_____

_____

_____

_____

Monitor your progress

What's the next step?

N.O.

N – Not

O – Optional

NO means NO! It's as simple as that and, when you say it, you need to mean it. Sometimes when you are told NO, you have a difficult time accepting it and your response is automatic. Because you are learning to do what is in your best interest (your standard of behavior), immediately engage in a coping skill that delays your reaction long enough for you to think about what you should do.

O

THE 'Ooops' FACTOR

Have you ever seen someone make a mistake and their response was "ooops". That response usually means that the mistake wasn't intentional. Once a mistake has been made, to continue making the same mistake takes away the 'ooops' factor and it becomes necessary for you to look at repetitive behaviors that may not be in your best interest.

Identify behaviors that continually cause you problems, but you continue to do them:

What skills can you use to help address these behaviors?

P

PERSONAL MAINTENANCE

Learning personal maintenance takes time but is very important to you becoming the best person you can be. It also expresses a level of maturity. Personal maturity is you doing the things you can do to make sure you are healthy, physical, mentally and socially.

Personal maintenance requires:

- Spending time with yourself daily in thought and meditation; at least 15-30 minutes

- An understanding of the behaviors that hurt or help you. Developing a plan to let go of the negative behaviors.

- Letting go of things and people that hinder your moving forward or reaching your goals.

- Celebrate small & large victories.

- Acknowledge mistakes and learn from the lessons that are embedded in your mistakes and failures.

Journaling is a great way for you to keep track of your advancement.

Create your maintenance plan: Take a moment and write down what you need to do to take care of yourself.

_____

_____

_____

_____

_____

_____

_____

_____

PERSONAL MAINTENANCE

Worksheet

What was your personal meditation today? _____

_____

_____

What negative behaviors are you trying to avoid today? ____

_____

_____

What are your plans for not engaging in those behaviors? ___

_____

_____

Which of your skills will you use to help you with your plan?

_____

_____

_____

What are the possible hinderances to meeting your goals today? _____

_____

_____

I will celebrate my victories today by: _____

_____

_____

The lessons I learned today were: _____

_____

_____

_____

P.O.W.E.R.

Power is something everybody wants at some point. It's the ability to be in control of a situation or a person in ways that are beneficial. What we don't want is for someone to have power over us. You must understand that you have the ability to keep or lose your personal power based on the choices you make.

How to keep your POWER:

P –   **Preparation** – Being prepared gives you an upper hand and helps you to be able to properly address situations you may face.

O –   **Organization** – Organization adds clarity and order. You think better when the things around you are laid out in a specific way.

W –   **Willingness** – This is a desire to do what you need to do to make your life and situations the best they can be.

E –   **Educate –** Knowledge is power, and education comes in so many different forms. Be eager to learn because it will always give you an advantage and it can be very enjoyable.

R –   **Resources –** Something or someone that can be drawn on for support or assistance. You should gather resources like a hobby. They are in unexpected places and always helpful. You never know when you're going to need them.

How to lose your POWER:

P –   **Procrastination –** Putting things off never gets things done! Regardless of your good intentions you will fall behind.

O –   **Obstinate –** Being stubborn works against you because it makes it difficult to take in information if it doesn't come the way you expected. It also become difficult to embrace change.

W –   **Wayward –** Moving away from the things you know are right to do. It's too easy to get off track, and to knowingly go in the wrong direction isn't wise!

E –   **Endangering –** Safety is vital!! Putting yourself in situations that are not safe physically, emotionally, or spiritually, is completely unacceptable and violates your **Standard of Behavior**.

R –   **Rejection –** Help is available, and everyone needs help to reach their full potential. When you don't accept help or instruction when it's offered, you're making things more difficult for yourself.

PROS & CONS

This skill is very easy and helps you to get some direction when looking at a situation that you're not sure of. Understand that the 'pros' represent reason in favor of something and the 'cons' are reasons to be against something.

Here's how you do it:

1.   Take a sheet of paper.
2.   Draw a line down the middle.
3.   At the top of one column write 'PROS'.

4. At the top of the other column, write 'CONS'.

5. Fill out each column.

There are two ways to sift through the information. Once gathered you can go through the information quickly, or you can take time to think about the information you have gathered. Base your decision on your **Standard of Behavior.**

Q

QUIET TIME

In a busy day there doesn't seem to be much opportunity for quiet time. The purpose of this time is to stop for a moment and breathe. It may be difficult in the beginning to make this a part of your routine; but you will find this to be one of the high points of your day.

Here are some suggestions for you to make your quiet time beneficial:

- A quiet place
- It must be at least 15 minutes
- No devices such as phones, laptops or anything that can take your focus away from your quiet time.
- Music is helpful; preferably soft and wordless.
- Paper and pencil

These are just suggestions. This is your time and you should develop it the way you need it to be. The only hard a fast rule is to minimize the distractions.

FIRST WEEK OF QUIET TIME:

Day 1

_____

_____

_____

Day 2

_____

_____

_____

Day 3

_____

_____

_____

Day 4

_____

_____

_____

Day 5

_____

_____

_____

Day 6

_____

_____

_____

Day 7

_____

_____

_____

QUESTIONS

Curiosity is a wonderful thing and questions are how we answer that curiosity. Questions are the way we gather information so that we can be more comfortable in different situations. Asking questions will take you on a quest/journey and learning how to ask the right question is an art form that takes practice. Who, what, when where, why and how are good starting points and from there you can start your journey to answers.

Ask one question and see how far you can take it:

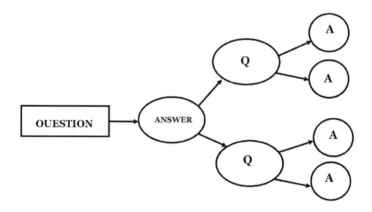

This quest could go on for a while because each answer produces additional questions. Don't be afraid to ask questions.

Q.S.S. (pronounce kiss)

Q.S.S. is a skill to be used to avoid moving too quickly in a situation or talking too quickly. It means:

Quick – Be quick to hear. Taking the time to hear will allow you to get an understanding of the situation you're in.

Slow – Slow to speak. Don't be in such a hurry to start talking. If you can take your time, you will be able to speak with a greater understanding.

Slow – Slow to anger. This takes practice but as you develop your skills, it will be easier to slow down any angry reaction.

R

REMOTE CONTROL

In the collecting of coping skills, it is important to use things that are familiar. What's more familiar than the buttons on any remote control? Here you will find such easily remembered skills:

Change the channel – Leave a negative situation for something better; this can be physically or mentally.

Menu/Schedule - Review what's coming and possible consequences.

Adjust volume – Adjust the volume to control a situation. Sometimes you get louder to get people's attention and make sure you're heard. Using quieter tones works the same way.

Turn off or on - Don't listen to instigating conversations. Engage/disengage.

Exit – Get out of the situation without any further interaction.

Rewind – Remember past mistakes and consequences.

Fast forward – Plan out your next move

Pause – Don't move (S.T.O.P.- silence, take deep breath, organize thoughts, proceed)

Mute – No sound. Don't say another word or make any noise.

Record – Analyze a situation gone wrong to see what you could have done differently.

R.E.S.P.E.C.T.

The first rule of 'respect' is to respect yourself. If you understand the value of self-respect, showing respect for others won't be difficult. If you violate your **Standard of Behavior,** you are disrespecting yourself.

The benefits of 'respect' are:

R – Rejuvenate - makes you feel good about yourself.

E – Encourage – increases your confidence

S – Success – achieving good results

P – Progress – forward movement

E – Elevate – lifts you to where you needs to be

C – Courageous – addressing fear and continuing

T – Teaches – enlightens.

To practice **RESPECT** as a skill, you treat others the way you want to be treated. As far as self-respect is concerned, one rule of thumb is that you never do anything that you don't want to see on a billboard.

RESPOND VS. REACT

If you are ever in a situation that has any level of conflict, you must understand that you have the choice to either 'react' or 'respond'. To react is emotion without thought. To respond is to think before you act.

RESPOND	REACT
Think things out	Moving automatically
Gives you P.O.W.E.R.	Takes P.O.W.E.R. away
Controllable outcome	Unwanted consequences
Allows for choices	Limits choices

S

SELF-CONTROL

Self-control comes about through practice. It is vital for your personal success and can be achieved by using the skills you are developing. Everyone develops at their own pace. As you have come through this book, you have been gathering different skill.

List the skills you feel will help you to gain and maintain self-control.

1. _____

2. _____

3. _____

4. _____

5. _____

The key to the skills is to use them on a regular basis. You will get better at using the skills only though practice.

SELF-ESTEEM

Mirror, mirror let me see

All the value within me.

May I see who I can be

And feel the joy of loving me.

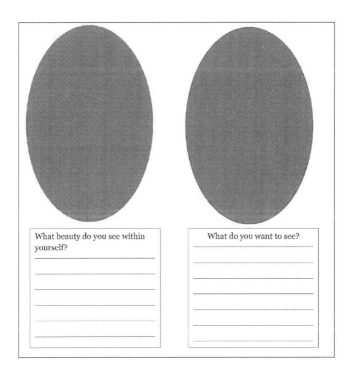

What beauty do you see within yourself?

What do you want to see?

- Self-esteem basically means how you feel about yourself. It also means how you judge yourself. your view of yourselves is developed from many different sources, such as: family, peers, media, spirituality, and what you tell yourself.

- It is necessary to continuously work on your self-esteem because how you see and judge yourself changes; sometimes without your knowledge.

- There are outside influences on your self-esteem, but you must understand that you have the ability to help yourself by doing things that strengthen you as an individual. It also means that you don't have to allow outside influences to negatively impact your self-view.

- There's an old saying, "chew the meat and spit out the bones". That is the attitude you need to improve your self-esteem or any other area of your life. When you are presented with information or suggestion, if it is helpful keep it and if not, let it pass you by.

For your own knowledge, complete this exercise. Identify two things that you need in these areas of your life that will boost your self-esteem.

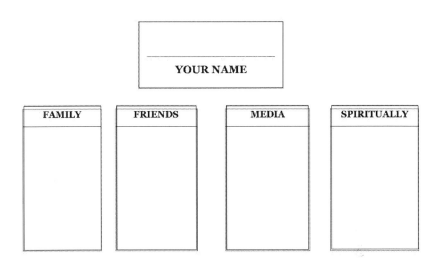

S.H.U.T. D.O.W.N

Shut Down is a skill that is used when you're feeling a little overwhelmed and you're trying to gather your thoughts to make a decision about what you need to do.

S – Silence - you can't hear when you're talking.

H - Hear what is being said - listen and understand what's being said.

U - Understand the options.

T - Time out – (quick moment to mentally get your thoughts together).

D – determine the right thing to do (in detail).

O – organize your thinking (filter question fit in here).

W – work out your plan.

N – navigate to appropriate plan

S.H.U.T. U.P.

This is not an attempt at being rude, but it means what it says. There are times when one more word will escalate the situation in a negative way. The best thing to do is to stop talking and go into skill mode.

S – Silence - you can't hear when you're talking.

H - Hear what is being said - listen and understand what's being said.

U - Understand the options.

T - Time out – (quick moment to mentally get your thoughts together).

U - Utilize coping skills - know what skill fits the situation.

P - Proceed with a plan.

S.T.O.P. & T.H.I.N.K.

S.T.O.P. & T.H.I.N.K. must become part of your collection of skills. Too often the difficulty you get into would not have occurred if you would have just taken a moment to think before you acted. Don't operate on automatic, take a moment to stop and think. Out of all the skills you are learning, this may be the most important one.

S – Silence. Stop talking and quiet your mind.

T – Take a deep breath. Take a moment to focus.

O – Organize your thoughts. What's happening in the moment? What do you need to do? What will your consequences be? (*This is a good place to use your filter questions*)

P – Proceed with a plan.

&

T – Take - means to move deliberately.

H – Honest – tell yourself the truth; not just what you wish.

I – Inventory – look closely at the situation and gather info.

N – Navigate – move with direction and determination.

K – Knowledge – based on the inventory, you know what to do.

Thinking is key, but the thinking must be purposeful and honest; lying to yourself defeats your purpose. When you inventory a situation, use the five W's and an H (who, what, when, where, why, how). Once inventory is taken you can begin to navigate; move forward using the knowledge you have gained.

STREET SIGNS

Here is another set of coping skills that are familiar and easy to remember. You see them on a regular basis and now they'll mean even more to you.

S.T.O.P. - Get **S**ilent, **T**ake a deep breath, **O**rganize your thoughts **P**roceed with a plan.

Yield - Allow the other person in the conflict to have a chance to voice their views and then you take your turn.

Exit - Take space and leave the situation without any further interaction.

'U' turn - See a negative situation ahead and go the other direction.

Speed bump - Slow yourself down, slow your breathing and conversation to allow yourself time to think.

Dead End - Realize that the conversation or situation isn't going anywhere and step away.

Do not enter - Don't instigate others. Don't say things that you know are going to cause further conflict.

Caution - Be aware of your surroundings.

Merge - Blend into the background. Don't be the one to keep drama going.

S.U.C.C.E.S.S.

Success is a goal that we strive for daily. You must know that success is achievable, but you must first know what success looks like for you. How will you know that you're successful if can't recognize it? Also, your success is yours and doesn't have to look like someone else's.

Describe what success looks like to you.

_____

_____

_____

_____

Here's a few tips to help you gain and maintain your success.

S - Set clear realistic goals.

> What do you want to achieve? If you're not exactly sure, start paying attention to what your options are. Then look for people who are doing what you want to do, write it down and keep notes on your process.

U - Understand what information you need to gather.

> Who? What? When? Where? Why? How? These questions are good starting points. Start general and then get specific.

C - Courage; not trying will insure failure.

This starts in the mind. You must begin and continue telling yourself positive things. Encourage yourself throughout the process. It may feel foreign in the beginning but use positive self-talk until it become second nature to you. ("I can do this")

C - Concentrate on the goal and your behavior.

Pay attention. Distractions come in all shapes and sizes. Even the most well intending person can become a distraction. Monitor the progress you're making toward the goal you set. What are you **doing** and what do you still need to **do**?

E - Engage; success begins with the first step.

The first step is the most difficult because you're stepping out of your comfort zone and putting into action things you've only thought about. Positive self-talk in vital at this point because negative thoughts and doubts will come without invitation. Remember that you're headed in a direction you want to be going in.

S - Speak your mind.

This is a time to speak up. Don't be so afraid that you're going to say something wrong, that you don't say anything. Asking questions and sharing your opinions is how you'll find out whether you're going in the right direction. However, don't just talk to anybody, talk to people who are like minded; trying to do something with their lives.

S - Selective; be selective about who you allow to influence you.

Create a strong support system. Include people who care about you and are able to tell you the truth. Select people who you know are smarter than you so that you can be challenged. Understand what each person brings to your life. There will be some 'friends' that you will have to distance yourself from in order for you to grow. Be your own first priority.

T

TIMEOUT

Timeouts can be life savers. The purpose of a **TIMEOUT** is to give you a moment to think clearly. It also serves to give you a little **relief** in a stressful situation.

Here are some simple 'Timeout' guidelines.

R – **Remove** yourself from the situation; preferably a quiet place.

E – **Evaluate** the situation and your anger on a scale of 1-10.

L – **Look** for the appropriate coping skill to use in the timeout.

I – **Identify** a possible solution to the situation.

E – **Evaluate** your anger and your ability to return to the situation.

F – **Fifteen** minutes away before returning to the situation.

Mild   midway point   intense

One on the ratings scale means mild and 10 is very intense. After using your coping skill, the number on the second evaluation should be below a five before you consider returning to the situation. If the timeout requires more than 15 minutes, you may have to return at another time to resolve the situation.

T.R.U.S.T.

Trust is valuable and should be treasured! It should not be given automatically; but earned. When it is violated it's difficult to get back.

- Try this exercise. Take a sheet of paper, and in large letters, write the word trust. Now rip it in half. Try putting it back together; not too difficult. Rip it in half four (4) more times; not so easy to put back together.

The more 'trust' is violated the more difficulty it is to fix; until it is impossible.

When you are trying to build or rebuild trust, remember these keys:

T – **Truth –** Telling the truth is absolutely a must. Lies corrodes trust.

R – **Reliable –** Be reliable. If you say you're going to do something, do it.

U – **Understand –** Understand the value of trust; cherish it.

S – **Show yourself worthy –** Why should you be trusted? Prove it!

T – **Time –** Realize that regaining trust takes time; it's a process.

U

UNDERSTANDING

When we talk about understanding as a skill, it simply means to take some time to see things from more than one perspective. You don't have to agree with other perspectives but at least you have an understanding of what's out there.

UNPLUG

UNPLUG is a self-preservation skill. You unplug when you've had enough, and it seem like you're being pulled in too many different directions. To unplug correctly you must take charge of your surroundings because it is very easy to become distracted.

U –   **Unwind –** Simple relaxation exercises using deep breathing.

N –   **Nurture –** Do something kind for yourself without feeling guilty.

P –   **Play –** Do something frivolous; just for the fun of it. Card game etc.

L –   **Listen –** Listen to something soothing; music or an audio book….

U –   **Understand –** Get an understanding of why unplugging was needed.

G –   **Gain –** Gain a new perspective in order to successfully plug back in.

To UNPLUG successfully, no texting, answering emails, running errands or anything else that prevents you from concentrating on yourself.

V

VICTORIES

Sometimes victories are hard to come by, and unless they are huge, we don't necessarily acknowledge them. It is important to acknowledge or maybe even celebrate your victories. This is particularly important if you're not in the habit of saying or doing positive things for yourself. This takes practice because sometimes we are more accustomed to noticing our negatives and not our positives.

Let's practice: Identify three (3) victories for three (3) days and the positive message you give to yourself.

Day 1:

Identify your victories	What is the positive message you gain from this victory?

Day 2:

Identify your victories	What is the positive message you gain from this victory?

Day 3:

Identify your victories	What is the positive message you gain from this victory?

VIRTUES

Virtues are not talked about much anymore, but they are more important than ever. Virtues are qualities or habits that enhance your character. Examples of virtues are: loyalty, honesty, dependability, respectful, compassion, generosity, empathy, patience, charity, kindness, courageous, forgiving; to name a few.

The great thing about virtues is that you can always improve on the ones you have, and you can gain the ones you desire to have.

How do you rate yourself in the virtue department?

Name your virtues	Not interested	Don't have but want	Could use some work	One of my best qualities

W

WATER SIPPING

This is a skill that can be used in a lot of different situation to help you to calm down and refocus. When you become angry one of the first things that happens to you is that your body temperature rises. In bringing down your body temperature, you also take some of the 'grrrrr' out of your anger. This skill works in combination with 'mind vacation' *(page 64)* and 'come to your senses' *(page 23)*.

Here are the steps for Water Sipping:

- Get a cold glass of water.

- Find a quiet place

- Wrap your hands around the glass and allow yourself to experience the coolness of the glass.

- Using the 'Mind Vacation' *(page 64)* skill, begin your journey by taking a sip of the cold water; paying close attention as the water goes down.

- Between each of the senses, take a sip of water until you've completed all five senses.

- You must continue sipping water until the water is gone

This skill allows you to focus on something other than the issue at hand; while giving you time to calm down.

WILLINGNESS

Willingness isn't necessarily a skill but a state of mind. In order to make any type of improvement in your life, there must be a willingness to do the necessary work so that you can enjoy a skillful life. Willingness also includes addressing the things that cause you to fear.

WORDS

Words have power! They are valuable tools with limitless possibilities. Words as tools starts with a small notebook in which you will collect your words. The words can come from anywhere and they can be any size.

When entering the word write a brief definition. Once you learn the word, try using it as much as possible for the next few days. Start your collection here.

New Word	Definition

X

X - FACTOR

Just like in mathematics, the 'X' factor represents the unknown. There are a lot of unknowns, but let's stay focused on unknown situations and skills. We are coming to the close of this book and if you started at the beginning, you have been introduced to quite a few skills. These skills will be useless if you don't understand which one to use in what situation. Practice is the only way to become better at appropriately using the skills. An additional element to factor into your skills equation is called the desired outcome. All these things put together create an equation.

SITUATION + COPING SKILL = DESIRED OUTCOME

Now create your own equations. Identify situations that you have had difficulty with, then identify your desired outcome. Once that's done, go through the skills that you are most familiar with and choose the one that will give you your desired outcome.

_____ + _____ = _____

_____ + _____ = _____

_____ + _____ = _____

_____ + _____ = _____

_____ + _____ = _____

Y

YOURSELF

Be **Yourself**. Learning to be yourself is an ongoing process for everyone. One of the keys to doing this is to be honest with yourself and be willing to learn life's lessons; even when they are difficult. Understand that you are 'fearfully and wonderfully' made. In other words, you are not a mistake. You are uniquely and intricately designed on purpose, and with purpose.

It is a waste of time to try being like someone else. They may have qualities that you admire but if you're focused on being like them, you're not giving yourself a chance to be the best 'YOU', you can be.

We go through different situations because there are lessons we need to learn; about ourselves and the world we live in. The real test of whether we've learned a lesson is how we put that lesson into practice.

What have you learned about friends?

_____

_____

_____

_____

How have you put that lesson into practice?

_____

_____

_____

_____

What have you learned about consequences?

_____

_____

_____

_____

How have you put that lesson into practice?

_____

_____

_____

_____

What have you learned about your behavior?

_____

_____

_____

_____

How have you put that lesson into practice?

_____

_____

_____

_____

What additional lessons have you learned and how are you using those lessons?

_____

_____

_____

_____

_____

_____

_____

_____

Z

ZEAL

Zeal is defined as: great energy, effort and enthusiasm. You have one life and you owe it to yourself to live it the best way that you can.

- **Energy = Power**
- **Effort = A determined attempt**
- **Enthusiasm = Excitement**

Zeal is what you need to live your life in a way that will make you proud of who you are. As with most things, this take practice. The good thing about zeal is that when you operate with zeal, it picks up momentum and becomes part of who you are.

Live Skillfully,

The end

Made in the USA
Columbia, SC
14 December 2018